# THE ISRAELI-PALESTINIAN CONFLICT

## By Cory Gunderson

WORLD IN CONFLICT

## VISIT US AT
## WWW.ABDOPUB.COM

Published by ABDO & Daughters, an imprint of ABDO Publishing Company, 4940 Viking Drive, Suite 622, Edina, Minnesota 55435.

Printed in the United States.

Edited by: Sheila Rivera
Contributing Editors: Paul Joseph, Chris Schafer
Graphic Design: Arturo Leyva
Cover Design: Castaneda Dunham, Inc.
Photos: Corbis, Fotosearch

### Library of Congress Cataloging-in-Publication Data

Gunderson, Cory Gideon.
     The Israeli-Palestinian conflict / Cory Gunderson.
       p. cm. -- (World in conflict--the Middle East)
     Includes index.
     Summary: Provides background information on the conflict between Jews and Palestinians that has lasted from Biblical times to present.
       ISBN 1-59197-416-X
         1. Arab-Israeli conflict--Juvenile literature. [1. Arab-Israeli conflict.]
         I. Title. II. World in conflict (Edina, Minn.). Middle East.

     DS119.7.G855 2003
     956.04--dc21

                                                                    200304038

# TABLE OF CONTENTS

Israeli citizens panic after a suicide bombing in Jerusalem.

# OVERVIEW OF A LONG CONFLICT

Both Palestine and Israel believe they have rights to the same land. The Palestinians say the Jews drove them out of their homeland. The Jews believe the land has been theirs since Biblical times. If they didn't have Israel as their homeland, Jewish people would consider all Jews homeless. They want a place that's uniquely theirs.

The current leaders of Israel and Palestine want peace. Most Israelis and Palestinians want peace. The two sides have come close. Still, a solution to their complex dispute has not been found.

Israel and Palestine are in the heart of the Middle East. They are between the Mediterranean Sea, Egypt, Jordan, Lebanon, and Syria. These two groups are fighting for control over the same territory. They have had boundary disputes for

LEBANON

*Hula valley & Nature Reserve*

SYRIA

Haifa

Nazareth

*Mediterranean Sea*

*Sea of Galilee*

SYRIAN DESERT

Tel Aviv-Yafo

Ramla

Jerusalem

Jericho

Bethlehem

Gaza

*Gaza Strip*

Hebron

*Dead Sea*

Be'er Sheva

ISRAEL

SAU
ARA

EGYPT
(Sinai Peninsula)

JORDAN

**A map showing the territory in conflict**

*Red Sea*

more than 50 years. Egypt, Syria, Iraq, Lebanon, and Jordan have all fought against Israel at some point. These countries support Palestine because they, too, are Arab.

Israel and Palestine are quite different from each other. Each has its own distinct culture and history. The official language spoken in each is different. Israel's population is largely made up of Jews. Palestine is made up of mostly Muslims. Most Middle Easterners are Muslim. Muslims are followers of the Islamic religion. Israel is the only nation in the region where most of the people are not Muslim. Israel is also unique because it is the only Jewish nation in the world.

The roots of the Israeli-Palestinian conflict go back hundreds of years. It has not been resolved to this day. Watch the news or read the newspaper and you will find words in the headlines such as "suicide bombers, assassinations, conflict, and killing." Even today the clashing between the Palestinians and the Israelis continues.

The Middle East conflict plays out in the headlines.

# HISTORY OF THE CONFLICT

I n Biblical times, the region now known as Palestine was known as Israel. It was located at the center of King Solomon's Jewish kingdom. The Jews and Arabs both speak Semitic languages. They have always lived in the region. There were centuries when the two ethnic groups did not fight each other. Both Jews and Muslims today consider key cities within Palestine to be holy cities.

During the first century A.D., the Roman Empire took over the area that they came to call Palestine. The Romans were Pagans. They clashed with the Jews and forced most of them out of the area.

During the nineteenth century, Britain, France, and the Turkish Ottoman Empire controlled most of Arabia. The Turks controlled Palestine. They controlled it from 1517 to 1917.

Europe

Black Sea

OTTOMAN EMPIRE

Caspian Sea

Mediterranean
Sea

ARABIAN EMPIRE

Mid

Africa

Red Sea

Ea

A map showing seventeenth century empires

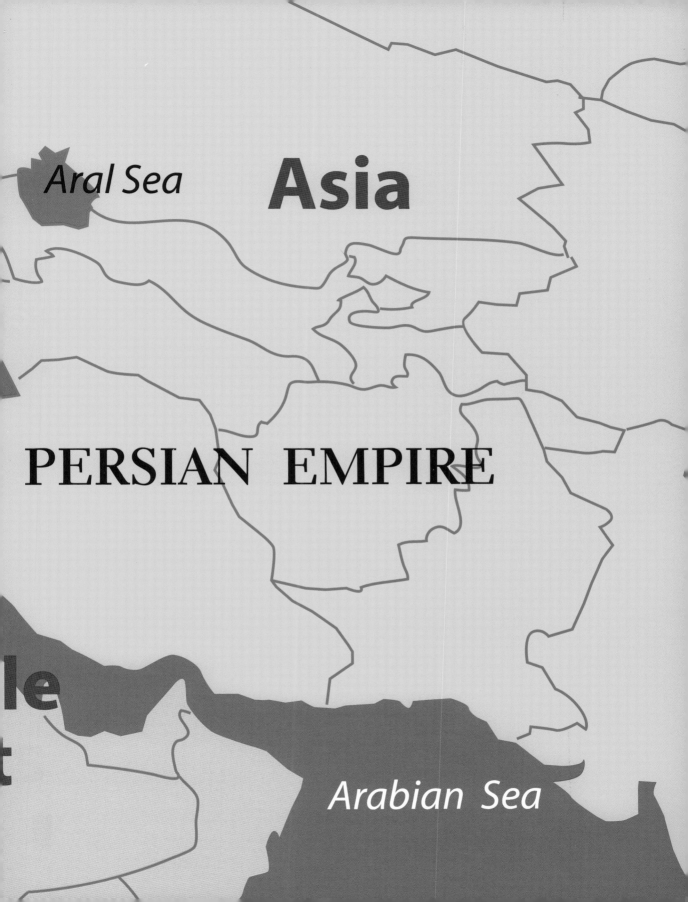

During this time, many of the Jewish people whose ancestors had been forced out of Palestine began to return. Eighty-five thousand Jewish people lived in Palestine by 1914. During the Ottoman Empire, Jewish people and Arabs lived together in peace.

The Ottoman Empire began to fall apart in the early twentieth century. During World War I, the British and Arabs fought together to defeat the Turks in Palestine. From 1920 until 1948, the British controlled Palestine. They planned to rule until the Palestinians could rule themselves. The British promised the Palestinian Arabs independence. They did this to thank them for their help in defeating the Turks.

Although the British government promised Palestinian Arabs independence, Arthur Balfour had already made other plans. Balfour was Britain's foreign secretary. He promised the Jewish people their own homeland.

In 1917, the foreign secretary drafted the Balfour Declaration. This promise established a homeland in Palestine for the Jews. It respected the non-Jewish settlers' rights, too. Details of each plan would not allow both promises to work. Tension between the Jews and Palestinians resulted in acts of violence between them. They both wanted the land for themselves.

Arthur Balfour, Britain's foreign secretary and author of the Balfour Declaration

In April 1936, the Palestinian Arabs began to attack Jewish and British targets. The three-year period of fighting that followed was called the Arab Revolt. The Arabs wanted to end Jewish immigration. They did not want to transfer any land to Jewish owners. They also wanted a new government to represent their needs.

The British attempted to make peace between the Jews and Arabs in Palestine. They formed a commission to help settle the two countries' disputes. The commission's purpose was also to inform the British government on how Palestine's government was developing.

In 1937, the Peel Commission's plan was presented to the British government. Members of the Peel Commission knew that tension and violence were increasing within Palestine. It proposed to set up two states. Their plan was to give a small part of the land in the north to the Jews. They would give a larger portion in the south to the Arabs. The British would rule the holy lands, eventually giving control of the cities to the Jews. The Peel Commission's plan contained many weaknesses.

While Jewish-Arab tension was growing in Palestine, Jews were being persecuted elsewhere. Jewish people in Europe suffered in countries that fell under Nazi influence. Jews who weren't forced into concentration camps were forced to flee their homes. Some countries limited the number of Jewish immigrants they would allow to enter. Other countries completely closed their borders. With few choices open to them, Jewish people poured into Palestine in increasing numbers. They sought refuge within its borders.

By 1947, there were 600,000 Jews living in Palestine. The increase in the Jewish population made the Palestinians concerned about their future. The violence increased.

By early 1947, the British decided that the Peel Commission plan would not work. Too many Arabs opposed it. Britain also felt pressured by Jews within Palestine and from the United States. Britain couldn't handle the tension. They turned the issue over to the United Nations (UN).

The UN is an organization of countries that work together for worldwide peace. In November 1947, a UN committee approved the Peel Commission Report. The majority of the committee accepted it as a reasonable solution to the Palestinian problem. The now British-opposed plan was presented to the

UN General Assembly.  The majority, including the United States and the Soviet Union, accepted it.

On May 14, 1948, the UN agreed to divide Palestine into two states.  On the eve of the announcement, the Jews decided to act on their own.  They declared themselves an independent nation.  The Jews called their nation "Israel."  Neighboring Arab nations rejected Israel as an independent nation.  On May 15, Egypt, Syria, Lebanon, Jordan, and Iraq declared war.  They attacked Israel on all borders in hopes of destroying the Jewish nation.  They believed they would achieve a victory in a short amount of time.  Israel's Arab opponents backed down one by one.  Only one year later did the fighting finally slow down.

Israel maintained its territory.  It even gained more land than the UN agreement allowed.  Though Israel won, the battle for Palestine was far from over.

# THE GAZA STRIP

**MEDITERRANEAN SEA**

Atey Sinai

Dugit

Nisanit

Al-Atatra

Erez

**Beit Lahiya**

Passage to the West Bank

Shati

**Jabaiya**

**GAZA**

Gaza Seaport

Nezarim

**An-Nuseriat**

Al-Mintar Crossing

**Bureij**

**Deir Al Balah**

**Al-Maghazi**

**ISRAEL**

Nezer Hazani Katif

Kfar Darom

Ganei Tai

Kissufim Crossing

Neve Dekalim

**Khan Yunis**

Pe'at Sade

Gadid Bedolah

av

Bne Atzmon

Morag

**Rafah**

Planned Industrial Zone

Sufa Crossing

## Legend

⬤ Palestinian cities, localities, and refugee camps

▢ Palestinian autonomous area

▲ Israeli settlements

— Settlement access road patrolled by Israel

- - - Disputed boundary of the Gaza Strip

**The Gaza Strip**

# PALESTINE

**P**alestine is a nation whose borders have changed throughout history.  Yasser Arafat currently leads the Palestinian Liberation Organization (PLO).  The PLO is the group that represents the people of Palestine.  The area currently called Palestine is made up of two pieces of land.  Both pieces fit within the larger area of Israel.  These areas are the Gaza Strip and the West Bank.

The Gaza Strip is a small piece of land bordering the Mediterranean Sea adjoined to Egypt.  The West Bank is a larger piece of land on the east side of Israel.  It borders the Jordan River, which separates it from the country of Jordan.

Palestinians consider both pieces of land theirs.  Yet they do not have complete control of them.  Palestinians have limited control of the Gaza Strip and the West Bank.  Both are occupied by Israeli military, and there are many Israeli settlements within them.  Many Palestinians live in refugee camps in the occupied territories.  Occupied territories are those that the Palestinians live in but are controlled by Israel. Some Palestinians live in neighboring countries.

The Palestinian people are primarily Arab. Arabs speak a language called Arabic. This language is widely spoken throughout the Middle East. Many, but not all, Arabic people share a common religion, which is Islam. Palestine has a mostly Muslim population, although a small percent is Christian.

The government of Palestine is loosely formed and based on Islamic principles. They have no formal military.

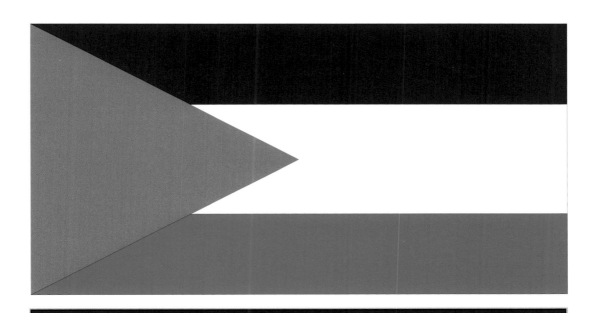

**The flag of Palestine**

# ISRAEL

Israel's official language is Hebrew, although its minority Arab population speaks Arabic. The Hebrew language was first spoken by the Jews in Biblical times. Today, English is the most commonly used foreign language.

Israel was designated to be a homeland for much of the world's Jewish population. The majority of Israelis practice Judaism, while small percentages practice Islam or other religions.

Israel's government consists of a legislature, a prime minister, a cabinet, and a president. The president is considered the head of state. He or she is elected by members of the legislature, which is called the Knesset, and his or her powers are limited. Any Israeli citizen can be elected President.

The prime minister leads the government and the cabinet. The prime minister must receive at least 50 percent of the votes to be elected into office. Citizens also elect members of the Knesset. The cabinet is appointed by the prime minister and approved by the Knesset.

Jerusalem from a distance

Israel's current prime minister, Ariel Sharon, was elected to office in 2001. During his campaign, he promised to work toward security in Israel.

The U.S. has been one of Israel's strongest supporters. The U.S. has given both political and military support to Israel throughout its rocky history. Because of its support for Israel, the U.S. has faced threats from Arab nations. Islamic extremists have targeted U.S. military sites and embassies to punish the U.S.

Israel has also received support from Britain and France. Jews from other countries have supported Israel as the homeland for all Jewish people.

Israel's military has been well organized and well equipped. In the late 1930s, Jews in Jerusalem created a military defense unit called "Haganah." Members of this unit trained themselves. Some trained with British police. They designed a defense plan that helped bring about their success in the war for independence.

# THE MODERN ISRAELI-PALESTINIAN CONFLICT

After the war for Israeli independence ended, Arab nations backed off. Still there was no peace for Israel. Many other wars have followed, including the Six Day War in 1967. In this war, Israel fought Egypt, Jordan, and Syria. The Arab forces received help from Iraq, Algeria, Kuwait, Saudi Arabia, and Sudan. The Israelis wiped out the air forces of each of those three countries and claimed victory. During the Six Day War, Israel took control of an area of Egypt called Sinai. They also took over the Golan Heights, the Gaza Strip, and the West Bank.

The UN called for a cease-fire, where both sides had to stop fighting. The war was over six days after it started. Israel gained more land from this war than from any other war.

Next came a war fought by Israel against Egypt and Syria. This war began on the Jewish holy day called Yom Kippur. It was called the Yom Kippur War. On October 6, 1973, Egypt and

An Israeli tank in the occupied territory

Syria waged a surprise attack on Israel. They wanted to take back the land they lost to Israel in the Six Day War. Egypt fought to retake control of the Sinai, and Syria tried to reclaim the Golan Heights. Israel maintained most of its territory. The war was over by the end of October.

Since these major wars in Israel, fighting between Israelis and Palestinians continued. Egypt and Israel battled over Sinai until the two sides came to an agreement in 1979. Israel agreed to return Sinai to Egypt. Before this agreement, Egypt refused to recognize Israel as a country.

One of the problems of the Israeli-Palestinian conflict was that many Palestinians had to flee Israeli territory. Some were forced out. These refugees had to immigrate to other countries. Many have had to live in refugee camps on the West Bank and the Gaza Strip. Some refugees live in camps in the surrounding countries of Lebanon, Jordan, and Syria.

Life as a refugee is not easy for Palestinians. People suffer in poor living conditions. Often there is not enough clean water. The roads are in poor shape, and there is overcrowding. Sometimes the Israelis treat these Palestinians as second-class citizens.

Living like this has caused Palestinians to feel connected to each other. The feeling of unity among Palestinians has led to

Yasser Arafat, leader of the Palestinian Liberation Organization (PLO)

the formation of various political groups. One of the biggest and most well known political groups is called the PLO.

The PLO was created in 1964 to represent Palestinians. One of its most influential members, Yasser Arafat, is also its current leader. It was reorganized in the late 1960s to include many Palestinian groups. Al Fatah and the Popular Front for the Liberation of Palestine are two of these.

The PLO's goal has been to defend Palestinians against Israeli forces. The group also wants to establish an independent Palestinian nation. During the 1970s, the PLO used violence toward Israelis to reach their goals. This violent approach would change. The PLO would eventually resolve conflicts by talking instead of fighting. The organization came to believe that a two-state division between Palestine and Israel was possible.

Another prominent Palestinian resistance group is called the Palestinian Islamic Jihad. The group was organized between 1985 and 1986. The Islamic Jihad feels that Palestinians must control all of Israel. It views all Jewish people as enemies.

Hamas is another Palestinian group fighting for Palestinian freedom from Israeli control. Hamas was created in late 1987. It is the largest and most widely supported Islamic movement in the Palestinian territories. Like the Islamic Jihad, Hamas' goal is to destroy Israel and establish Palestine as a Muslim nation. Hamas approves of violence against Israel. Murder and self-sacrifice are common ways to oppose Israel.

Hamas is also known for its political efforts. The group has created charities and spread leaflets and propaganda to the Palestinian people. They have also made other efforts to improve the lives of their displaced people.

**This way to Jerusalem, a holy city in dispute**

Israel tightened its control on the West Bank and Gaza. Palestinians had no rights as citizens. It was difficult for Palestinians to earn a living. More and more Israelis moved into Palestinian territory. In 1987, Palestinians living in the occupied territories began to revolt against the poor conditions under which they were forced to live. This revolt was called the Intifada.

These Palestinian revolts took the form of demonstrations, riots, throwing stones, and not paying taxes. The Israelis responded by arresting and sometimes killing Palestinians. Deaths and disappearances of Palestinians were not considered unusual. In November 1988, the Intifada died down when Palestinian leaders declared a Palestinian state. They said Jerusalem would be their capital and elected Yasser Arafat as president. In May 1989, Israeli officials agreed to discuss the development of a Palestinian government.

In 1993, Yasser Arafat held peace talks with former Israeli Prime Minister Yitzahk Rabin. They came to an agreement about the land. Although they signed the agreement, Israelis continued to control the Palestinians. In the end, tensions and a Hamas attack broke down the peace process.

Conflict erupts in Israel almost constantly. Both Israel and Palestine fight for their independence. Both nations have

An Israeli soldier aims his sniper rifle as fighting erupts in the West Bank.

experienced great losses in the fighting. Neighboring Arab nations have also suffered when they supported Palestine. Although the fighting continues, there have been peace talks and treaties along the way. The U.S. and other countries have hosted several of these.

The peace agreements usually call for Israeli military withdrawal from certain territories. They may open up waterways and require nations to improve refugees' living conditions. A representative from the UN may be assigned to help both sides achieve peace.

Some portions of some agreements have worked. Still, there is tension in the Middle East. The West Bank and Gaza continue under partial Israeli control. There are still thousands of Palestinian refugees living in camps. Political groups in Israel and Palestine continue to disagree. Major problems remain to be solved in the Israeli-Palestinian conflict.

# THE FIGHTING TODAY

**E**ven today, individuals and groups continue to oppose one another in Israel. Most everyone's goal is peace. Still, it will be difficult to decide who will control what land. Some involved in the Israeli-Palestinian conflict have proposed dividing the land in two. Yasser Arafat and Israeli leaders agreed to Palestinian control of the West Bank and the Gaza Strip. Yet Hamas stands opposed to giving any of the original Palestinian land to Israel.

Without an agreement by all, solutions seem impossible. Palestinians continue to fight the Israelis for independence. Israel continues to respond in defense. Violence continues as one group attacks, and the other fights back. Neither side is willing to compromise.

Israel and Palestine are still fighting today for the same reason that they originally fought. The two groups are divided along religious lines. In the end, though, the heart of the issue is ownership of the land. Neither side wants to continue the bloodshed that has haunted them for decades. Both sides, though, continue to believe in their right to the land. Both sides continue fighting for it. Peace is difficult when neither side is willing to compromise and violence continues to erupt.

**The Wailing Wall, or Western Wall, is a holy Jewish site.**

Israeli Prime Minister Ariel Sharon

Israel's Prime Minister Ariel Sharon would like to end the fighting that has hurt the country for years. In his 2001 election campaign, the prime minister stated that his priority was the security of Israel more than it was peace.

Palestinians lack trust in Sharon because of his involvement in the 1982 invasion into Lebanon. At the time of the invasion, Sharon was Israel's Defense Minister. Sharon's goal was to wipe out the PLO's power. Even after the Israeli army had the PLO under control, Sharon ordered more military attacks. The Israeli military killed hundreds of Palestinians living in refugee camps in Lebanon. Those killed were not soldiers. They were ordinary citizens.

The Lebanon invasion is not the only violence started by Israelis under Sharon's authority. Since Sharon became Prime Minister in 2001, Israeli forces have targeted Palestinians by bulldozing their farms and homes. They've also targeted members of various Palestinian political groups.

Throughout 2001 and 2002, Israel continued to retaliate against Palestinian uprisings with acts of violence. They killed members of Al Fatah and Hamas. The Israelis also used military force in lands controlled by the Palestinian National Authority. They attacked Palestinian police stations and invaded Palestinian towns and refugee camps.

Like Sharon, Palestinian President Arafat continues to seek an end to the conflict with Israel.  Although in its early days the PLO supported violent tactics, Arafat and the PLO support a peaceful approach to resolving the conflict.  In 1994, Arafat received the Nobel Peace Prize.

In early 2002, Arafat was placed under house arrest for several months by Israeli forces.  In May of 2002, he signed the Palestinian National Authority Basic Law.  The law bases Palestinian government on Islamic Shari'a Law.  It declares Palestine as part of a larger Arab Nation.

Hamas continues to oppose Israeli occupation of Palestinian land. Their involvement in the conflict has included suicide bombings and terrorist attacks.

Like Hamas, Islamic Jihad opposes the division of Israel into Palestinian and Israeli states.  Islamic Jihad wants the complete liberation of all of Palestine.  They have also used violence as a means to gain the attention of political leaders.  Islamic Jihad has been responsible for numerous terrorists attacks.

It is these acts of violence by political groups and individuals that makes peace difficult, if not impossible.  Sharon and Arafat may both be sincere in their desire to end the conflict.

Peace, though, will require the support of all Israelis and Palestinians. Sharon and Arafat cannot always control their citizens, and both want peace on their own terms.

Israel has received support from the United States for many years. U.S. President George W. Bush spoke to the UN General Assembly in September 2002. He seemed more balanced in his support. He talked about an end to the fighting. He also said, "America stands committed to an independent and democratic Palestine, living side by side with Israel in peace and security. Like all other people, Palestinians deserve a government that serves their interests and listens to their voices."

Israel reacted negatively to Bush's speech. They reoccupied the areas of the West Bank and Gaza with the exception of the city of Jericho.

Bush had more to say on the subject. He announced on March 14, 2003, that he would reveal his plan for the Middle East once a new Palestinian prime minister with real authority took office.

As long as militant groups rally against each other in Israel, no one knows when or how the two sides will achieve peace. Hope is hard to come by for both the Israelis and the Palestinians.

Israeli soldiers

# FAST FACTS

- Israel's current population is 80 percent Jewish. The remaining 20 percent of the population is mostly Arab; the Arabs are either Muslim or Christian.

- Almost all Palestinians are Muslim, or people who practice the religion of Islam.

- During the 1890s, European Jews began the Zionist movement. Its goal was to create a nation just for the Jewish people.

- By 1914, 85,000 Jews lived in Palestine. By 1947, 600,000 Jews lived there.

- Sympathy for the Jewish people increased after the Holocaust, and the push for a Jewish homeland grew stronger. In response to the Holocaust, more and more Jews wanted to enter Palestine.

- Al Fatah was founded by Yasser Arafat in 1957 to fight for the Palestinians and to take back the land that Israel had captured. Arafat and Al Fatah joined the PLO in 1968.

- During the Yom Kippur War in 1973, some Arab nations punished the United States for its support of Israel. These nations refused to sell the U.S. oil. This caused U.S. oil prices to soar.

- Palestinian President Yasser Arafat won the Nobel Peace Prize in 1994 for changing the focus of the PLO from military action to diplomatic efforts.

# TIMELINE

| | |
|---|---|
| **70 A.D.** | The Roman Empire takes control of Jerusalem. Most Jews are forced out. |
| **1517** | The Turkish Ottoman Empire takes control of Palestine. They control it until 1917. |
| **1917** | Britain issues the Balfour Declaration, which establishes a national homeland for the Jews. |
| **1936–1939** | The Arab Revolt. |
| **1937** | The Peel Commission plan is issued by Britain. It proposes how Israel and Palestine could find a lasting settlement. |
| **1947** | The British realize the Peel Commission plan can't work. Britain asks the United Nations to resolve the conflict. Jews and Arabs in Palestine battle. |
| **1948** | The UN agrees to divide Palestine into two states. Israel declares itself an independent nation. Egypt, Syria, Lebanon, Jordan, Saudi Arabia, and Iraq declare war on Israel. |

| | |
|---|---|
| **1949** | Israel and the Arab states agree to peace. Israel gains more land than the UN allotted it. |
| **1964** | The Palestinian Liberation Organization (PLO) is founded. |
| **1967** | After the Six Day War, Israel gains more land than it has gained in any other war. |
| **1969** | Yasser Arafat is elected chairman of the PLO. |
| **1973** | Yom Kippur War. Egypt and Syria wage a surprise attack on Israel. |
| **1978** | Egypt and Israel sign a peace treaty. |
| **1996** | Arafat becomes first president of Palestine. |
| **2001** | Ariel Sharon becomes prime minister of Israel. |
| **2003** | President George W. Bush announces on March 14, that he will reveal his plan for peace in the Middle East once a new Palestinian prime minister with real authority takes office. |

A scene from the Gaza Strip

# WEB SITES
## WWW.ABDOPUB.COM

Would you like to learn more about the Israeli-Palestinian Conflict? Please visit www.abdopub.com to find up-to-date Web site links about the Israeli-Palestinian Conflict and the World in Conflict. These links are routinely monitored and updated to provide the most current information available.

**Middle Eastern children**

# GLOSSARY

**Arab:**

Someone who speaks Arabic. Most Arab people are Muslim.

**Arabic:**

Language spoken by Arab people.

**Arafat, Yasser:**

Leader of the Palestinian Arabs.

**assassination:**

To kill a political leader.

**Balfour Declaration:**

Statement named after British foreign secretary, Arthur Balfour. It established a homeland for the Jewish people.

**fundamentalist (extremist, absolutist, radical):**

Person who believes in a traditional, usually severe or militant, version of religion.

**Gaza Strip:**

Narrow strip of land along the Mediterranean Sea near the city of Gaza, located within the boundaries of Israel.

**Haganah:**

Jewish military defense force that became the basis of the Israeli Army.

**Hamas:**

Militant Palestinian Muslim group.

**Holocaust:**

The Nazi attempt to kill all Jews living in German controlled land.

**Holy Land:**
Land that is considered sacred by a religious group.

**immigrate:**
Entering a foreign country to live.

**Intifada:**
The Palestinian uprising against the Israelis.

**Islamic Jihad:**
Group of fundamental Muslims that is against Israel.

**Israel:**
A Middle Eastern country established in 1948.

**Jewish:**
A person whose religion or culture is based on Judaism.

**Knesset:**
Israel's parliament.

**Koran:**
The Islamic holy book that contains the teachings of the prophet Muhammad.

**Middle East:**
Countries of southwest Asia and northeast Africa.

**Muslim:**
A believer of Islam.

**Nobel Peace Prize:**
A highly visible award that goes to a person who works to promote peace.

**occupied territory:**
Territory conquered by Israel.

**Palestine:**
A historical region of southwest Asia.

**Palestinian National Authority:**
The governing body of Palestine.

**Palestinian Liberation Organization (PLO):**
Main organization that represents Palestinian Arabs.

**Peel Commission:**
A royal British group that tried to negotiate a settlement between Palestine and Israel.

**Prime Minister:**
The person who holds the position of head of state in certain countries.

**refugee:**
A person who flees their homeland because of unsafe conditions there.

**Sharon, Ariel:**
Israeli prime minister who was elected in 2001.

**Six Day War:**
Arab nations battled Israel. Israel claimed victory after six days.

**United Nations (UN):**
The 191 nations that form an organization to promote peace around the world.

**Western nations:**
Countries in the western hemisphere and Europe where the population is typically Christian majority.

**Zionism:**
Movement to establish a Jewish state in Palestine.

More encouragement for violence

# INDEX